My Five Senses

WHAT I TOUCH

By Alex Appleby

Gareth Stevens
PUBLISHING

Please visit our website, www.garethstevens.com. For a free color catalog of all our high-quality books, call toll free 1-800-542-2595 or fax 1-877-542-2596.

Library of Congress Cataloging-in-Publication Data

Appleby, Alex.
What I touch / by Alex Appleby.
p. cm. – (My five senses)
Includes index.
ISBN 978-1-4824-0823-2 (pbk.)
ISBN 978-1-4824-0824-9 (6-pack)
ISBN 978-1-4824-0826-3 (library binding)
1. Touch – Juvenile literature. 2. Senses and sensation – Juvenile literature. I. Appleby, Alex. II. Title.
QP451.A66 2015
612.8–d23

First Edition

Published in 2015 by
Gareth Stevens Publishing
111 East 14th Street, Suite 349
New York, NY 10003

Editor: Ryan Nagelhout
Designer: Andrea Davison-Bartolotta

Photo credits: Cover, p. 1 iStock/Thinkstock; p. 5 michaeljung/Shutterstock.com; p. 7 Jupiterimages/Pixland/Thinkstock; p. 9 sonya etchison/Shutterstock.com; p. 11 Vinogradov Illya/Shutterstock.com; pp. 13, 24 (tongue) Pashin Georgiy/Shutterstock.com; p. 15 bikeriderlondon/Shutterstock.com; p. 17 paulaphoto/Shutterstock.com; pp. 19, 24 (door) DmitriMaruta/Shutterstock.com; p. 21 Dasha Petrenko/Shutterstock.com; pp. 23, 24 (ice) Brykaylo Yuriy/Shutterstock.com.

Printed in the United States of America

CPSIA compliance information: Batch #CS15GS: For further information contact Gareth Stevens, New York, New York at 1-800-542-2595.

Contents

Touch is my favorite sense.

I touch with my hand.

I touch my friend
Jack's hand.
This is a high five!

I pet my cat Betty.
She is very soft.

11

She licks my hand.
Her tongue is rough!

I touch some glue.
It is sticky.

I touch an apple.
It is very smooth.

I touch a door.
It is hard.

I touch the rain.
It is wet.

21

I touch some ice.
It is really cold!

Words to Know

door

ice

tongue

Index

24